CAREER IN JOURNALISM

A BEGINNER'S GUIDE TO BECOMING A JOURNALIST

ANTHONY EKANEM

Copyright © Anthony Ekanem
All Rights Reserved.

ISBN 979-888521706-4

This book has been published with all efforts taken to make the material error-free after the consent of the author. However, the author and the publisher do not assume and hereby disclaim any liability to any party for any loss, damage, or disruption caused by errors or omissions, whether such errors or omissions result from negligence, accident, or any other cause.

While every effort has been made to avoid any mistake or omission, this publication is being sold on the condition and understanding that neither the author nor the publishers or printers would be liable in any manner to any person by reason of any mistake or omission in this publication or for any action taken or omitted to be taken or advice rendered or accepted on the basis of this work. For any defect in printing or binding the publishers will be liable only to replace the defective copy by another copy of this work then available.

Contents

Preface

A great many people who want to be writers say that they want to have a career in journalism. They may envision themselves going to exotic locales to cover stories. While these things do happen to journalists, it takes a long time to make your bones before you are sent on any interesting assignments.

I became a journalist purely by accident. Unlike others who seek out journalism as a career, I wanted to be a writer. I envisioned myself writing books of fiction and entertaining the masses. My parents talked me into going to college and getting a degree in journalism. They told me that it was a good idea to have something to fall back on, in case I couldn't make a living writing fiction for a living. Five years and 100 rejections later, I realized they were right. Fortunately, my degree in journalism helped me support myself so that I didn't have to go back home after I got out of school.

I had no idea what a journalist did until I got my first job at a local paper when I was still in school. I was hired as a stringer and had to report on meetings. It was boring, but it paid for extras. Someone said that I was a journalist and I realised that I was working in a field for which I was studying.

A journalist is someone who reports on timely events. Timing is everything to a journalist. Whether you write for a periodical or a newspaper, you need to make sure that your articles are timely. Your purpose is to keep the public as up to date as possible when it comes to news and events that may affect them. This is the basic concept of being a journalist.

Since I became a journalist, I have made many mistakes. I've broken the rules a few times but learned lessons from each rule that I broke. It has taken me six years since I first started getting paid for my writing as a journalist, but in that time, I have become a good journalist. While my assignments are not exotic, I make a decent living and do something that I really enjoy.

If you are thinking about becoming a journalist, you must remember that the following rules apply:

1. **Impartiality**

You should report on all sides of a story, not just take one side, even if it appears that one side is right or wrong. A good journalist gets all sides of the story, prints it and then lets the reader decide, based upon the article. A good journalist does not make up the reader's mind for them.

2. **Timeliness**

Your stories must be timely. You do not have a compelling story about something that happened 20 years ago unless it can relate to what is happening now. Journalism is in the now - the immediate present. You must relate even historic pieces to what is happening right now.

3. **Facts.**

There is an old saying in journalism that still is used in the field today that states ***"If your mother says she loves you, check it out."*** Check and re-check your facts. Be sure that you double-check on names and spelling as well.

If you get to know and follow these three rules, your career in journalism will be very successful. If you break the rules - don't worry. I've broken all of them and I'm still standing. Just don't do it again. Some people like to learn in a trial by ordeal. I am one of them. But if you consistently break the golden rules of journalism, your career will suffer.

As a journalist, it is your job to reveal information to the public. This should be impartial, timely and truthful. To get into the computer system of the first journalism job that I had, the password was "truth." You must write the truth of what you see and hear and let the public form an opinion. You need to always quote sources when you are writing a journalism piece as you should not attribute anything to your own knowledge. Your articles should be written from a third-person point of view and from the outside looking in.

As you continue in your career, you will find your voice when it comes to your writing. Do not be surprised if your first articles are rewritten by your editor. Another rule that you need to learn when you are starting a career as a journalist is to not fall in love with your work. Do not feel hurt if an editor does not like a phrase in your article or makes some changes. They are only doing their job. You will soon get to know the editor and they will get to know your style of writing.

A journalist usually gets a job as a news reporter, and both news reporting and journalism are interchangeable careers. While many people think of journalists as writing on top stories or features all over the world, the education that you need to become a newspaper reporter and to be a writer for a magazine is the same - a degree in journalism. Anyone who writes an impartial article, be it news or feature stories, is practising journalism. If you choose to have a career in journalism, you will most likely get many different assignments in your career. The basic rules of journalism apply to everything that you write.

Many people feel that newspaper reporters only report the news and give more credit to journalists as they investigate the news - this is not true. Most newspaper reporters do a fair share of investigation into their stories or should. Those who report on crimes in the area and court actions are usually editors who have done their fair share of investigating in their stories. You will quickly learn when you are embarking on a career in journalism, which the more you investigate a story, the better the story will be. Sometimes you have time to do this, other times you are working on a tight deadline.

You should be able to work on a tight deadline when you are a journalist. Not only is this important if you are writing news stories, but it is also great training for any writer. The more you write, the more concise your work will become and the better quality you will be able to churn out in record time.

If you are interested in being a journalist, sit back and start reading. This book will tell you everything you need to know about becoming a journalist and making a living writing - both online and offline.

CHAPTER ONE

What Type of Degree Do I Need?

If you are serious about becoming a journalist, then you need to go to school so that you can get a job in this field. Newspapers and online venues are looking for those who have a four-year liberal arts degree in journalism. If you plan to get a job in the field, you need an education. While you can get some jobs reporting for local papers without a degree, you will never move up in the world unless you have that piece of sheepskin that says that you went to college to study journalism - no matter how talented you are as a writer.

There are journalism schools everywhere. You should apply to colleges that offer a bachelor's degree in Journalism, such as a good liberal arts college. Generally, the more prestigious the college, the more prestigious the job when you get out, although things are rapidly changing as the internet has become a formidable competition for the print media today.

Many journalists who want to have a career in the news industry will also minor in broadcasting. This can be helpful if you end up being a television journalist. A television journalist will go to a news scene and report about it live on the air. To be successful at this type of journalism, you need to have experience in telling the story, as well as broadcasting.

The Types of Journalism

Chances are that you are going to dabble in all the types of journalism that are out there. When you first start your career, you are going to want to take any job that you can get. Some of the journalist careers that you might consider include:

- Newspaper reporter
- Magazine writer
- Internet journalism
- Television reporter

These are the main types of journalism careers that you can get if you study journalism in school. You will most likely start as a newspaper reporter or work for an internet publication. Not only will employers want to see a degree, but they will also want to see clips. Clips are a portfolio of your work that indicates your byline. You can build up your portfolio in many ways that we will be discussing in a later chapter.

While you may be able to become a newspaper reporter on a lower level or even an internet journalist without a degree, you will need a degree in journalism if you want to become a magazine writer or television reporter. These are the more glamorous jobs that people think about when they imagine life as a journalist.

The bottom line is that if you want to be a serious journalist and have an option to move into an exciting career, go to school. Earn a BA in Journalism and you will be all set to start your career in journalism with nothing holding you back.

CHAPTER TWO

Writing Before Graduation

So, you have made up your mind to be a journalist and have enrolled in school. Congratulations! That is the first step towards carving out a career for yourself in the world of journalism. But do not think that you are going to walk out of college and land the dream job of working for a travel magazine and taking exotic trips. It doesn't work that way.

Before anyone will hire you full time, you are going to need experience. This is just the same thing as any other college graduate who finds it difficult to land a job without experience. This is why students often intern while in college - to gain experience. The good news about a career in journalism is that your internship can pay.

While some of my friends interned at larger city newspapers that are now out of business or heading that way, I decided to get a job as a stringer for my local paper. I commuted to college, so I had evenings free. I went to the editor of the paper and asked for a job. And just like that, he gave me one. Although I was still in school and had not earned my degree in journalism, I had clips to show him. After he read my clips, he said that he could hire me to work on a part-time basis, covering meetings. This was a part-time job that paid a little bit more than minimum wage, but I was glad to get it. I was getting a byline and experience working as a newspaper reporter.

I imagined myself covering all sorts of crime and corruption in my town, even though there wasn't much of either. Instead, I found myself sitting at school board meetings, township meetings, zoning board meetings and other municipal meetings that were boring. And they seemed like they lasted for hours, although they only lasted at the most, two hours. I had to report on what was going on and then send it to my editor that night. I didn't have a lot of time to mull over the story.

There was no set schedule for me at first, although as time went on, I began to go to the same meetings repeatedly. I got to know people who were leaders in the community as well as others. I got to understand the issues. People would usually come to the meeting with complaints, and I would have to write about it. Often, they called me a few minutes before they needed me to go out if no one else on staff could go. The most exciting thing that happened to me was to go to a reported fire at a nearby restaurant. It turned out that the fire was merely faulty fans and by the time I got there, all the fire trucks were gone, and everyone was eating at the restaurant. I still managed to get a story out of it, but not the story I imagined.

That is what life is like being a stringer. When I worked at this job, I found that a great many people worked as stringers for part-time pay or additional income. Most of them did not have a journalism degree. While we were technically on the payroll for the newspapers we were with, we did not have the same perks as those who were either part-time writers or full-time writers. We were not considered to be "real "reporters, but stringers. But having only a couple of hours to write a news story was the best experience that I ever had when it comes to writing.

Much has changed since then. A great many papers, even local ones, are cutting their staff. They are not putting anyone else on the payroll. But you can still get a job as a stringer. Freelance reporters are in high demand. Newspapers still need content to keep the news going, they just don't want to pay benefits to anyone who is on the staff. Being a freelance, or contractor for a newspaper will usually net you money per story. Some papers pay by word count, hours, or a flat rate for the story. This is a job that you can still get at print newspapers, although many print newspapers are closing their doors since people would rather get their news from the internet.

You can also write on the internet for money and build up a series of clippings that you can print out for your portfolio. The internet is the way of the future when it comes to journalism. The only problem with internet writing is that it tends to be a bit sloppy as compared to media print. This is because internet news is published right away, after a quick job of proofreading and sometimes, editing. As time wears on, however, and internet news becomes more influential, look for it to be a bit more polished.

There are also sites online that can help you earn money writing before you graduate. Such sites like Elance and Guru are a good way to get your foot in the door and start earning money for your writing. The only problem with these sites is that you will most likely be doing ghostwriting. While it will pay some bills, it does not afford you the byline.

There are many different news outlets online where you can apply for jobs. You will earn about $50 per article if you are accepted. They will want to see copies of your work before you get started. Some of them will test you out so that they can see if you can write in the style that they like.

There are sites like Associated Content, where you can get a few dollars for an article and get a byline. This is a good way to get started writing and they are one of the few legitimate companies online that pay you for your work. You will not earn a lot of money when you write for them, but you will be helping yourself build your portfolio.

Another option is to write for free. See if your local paper has an opening for a columnist, movie critic or other types of writers who are willing to write for free. This will not pay you anything, but it will get your name out there.

Although the newspaper was the first job that I got paid for, I did have another job that led to my getting the newspaper job. A small shopper paper was looking for a columnist that could talk about what was going on in the town. I sent them a sample of what I would write as I had no clips and they accepted me. I used these clips to get the newspaper job so that they could see a sample of my writing.

Even if you are still in school and have no degree, you can make money writing and gain experience at the same time. It is important that you start to gain experience in the field right away, paid, or unpaid, so that you have a better chance of getting a job once you finish college. Look at all avenues and do not forget to look at your local paper.

Most papers today are only too glad to get freelance writers as they do not have any employer obligation towards them. You will have deadlines and will have to teach yourself how to write quicker. You must be able to write quickly and concisely when you are working as a journalist and there is no better training than working as a newspaper reporter. There is no better training for being any type of writer than working in a newspaper. You do not have to have a degree to be a stringer - you can look for a job by talking to your local newspaper editors.

CHAPTER THREE

The Rules of Journalism

Earlier, I talked about the rules of journalism. That your stories need to be timely. That they must be fact-checked. That they must be unbiased. Other rules are not to fall in love with your own work and, of course, to always quote your sources. At one time or another, I broke all these rules! I'm going to give you examples of the rules, how I broke them and what should be done in the same situation.

1. Timely news stories. This was something that I couldn't get through my head for the longest time. An example of how I broke this rule was that a lawyer in our town was caught dealing drugs to kids. He was arrested and put in jail, a bond set. That was as much as we knew with our sources. My job was to call the police department, find out as much as I could about the current situation and then write a story about it. I had a two-hour time span to do this.

My story came out with the usual "who, what, when, where and how," which is standard in newspaper writing. But it wasn't timely. The man was arrested on a Friday, but the time I got the assignment it was Sunday, and our paper was going to press on Monday and coming out on Wednesday. Nearly a week after the arrest. My story, which detailed the arrest that was made a week prior was not timely.

The editor got the story and changed the first line. Instead of talking about the nearly week-old arrest, he described the man sitting in jail, as of the date we wrote the story, and waiting for a bond hearing. It brought the story up to date for the readers who would be getting the paper 6 days after the arrest was made. Not only that, but it also made the story more interesting.

High school journalism taught me about putting everything in the first sentence that was relevant to the story because, as my teacher said, "people have the attention span of gnats." But as I moved on in my journalism career, I saw that while the specifics are crucial to the story and should be in the first paragraph, they do not have to be all crammed into the first sentence. The purpose of the article should be to catch the attention of the readers and get them to read.

When writing any type of article for publication, look to how it affects the here and now for people. People are not going to want to read an article in which the events are old news. Bring it right to the current time frame and people will be more interested as it is up to date and providing them with real news.

You never see a story about something that happened weeks, months or even years ago without the most current update to the situation being discussed in the first paragraph. A relatively recent example was the story that broke on the kidnapping and murder of Adam Walsh. When this occurred nearly 30 years ago, it was big news. But as horrific as this crime was, you only saw an article about it when something new developed in the case. The most recent was the police closing the case and naming the likely murderer, who died in prison for another crime. That was news that was timely and was included in the headline and first paragraph of the story, as well as subsequent paragraphs. The story went back in time and then retold the kidnapping and murder of the child.

A good way to be timely in your news stories is to create a backwards timeline. Think of the last occurrence in the case and then work backwards from there. Always keep your articles up to date for your readers so that they can relate to them in the now.

2. Fact checked. Another rule I broke had more of a serious impact. My editor told me about a car accident where a young man who lived in our town was hurt and in the hospital. He told me to call the hospital and find out his condition. I was busy doing something else and time lapsed. I did try to call the hospital but could not get through to anyone who knew anything about the case. I did not try to employ any strategy to check my facts and wrote the story as if the boy was still in the hospital and recovering from a car accident.

This was a huge mistake because the boy died. And when a woman called up to complain about how we wrote such an article that was inaccurate and most likely painful for the parents to read, I got called out on the carpet. I told the editor part of the truth and that was that I could not get anyone to verify any part of the story. I was in trouble, but not for long. He admonished me with the old saying "remember, if your mother says she loves you, check it out." After that episode, I always made sure that I checked my facts before handing anything in for print.

There were several ways that I could have gotten the information that I wanted. I could have called neighbours and asked them the condition of the boy. I could have told the nursing station that I was a relative. I could have asked for his room at the switchboard. If there was no room, I would have known that there was something wrong. I could have asked a nurse which funeral home he was going to because I wanted to send flowers, presuming that he was dead. In short, I could have done my homework and exhausted all efforts to find out what I needed to know for that article, even calling relatives of the boy. But I took the lazy way out and paid the consequences.

At the very least, if I didn't want to resort to trickery to get the story, I could have told the truth from my perspective and that was that the boy's condition was unknown.

Always check your facts. Verify them and get someone to go on record, if possible. You do not have to name names, although you should be able to give the title of the person who told you the information. If I had found out the information about this boy, for example, I would have written that a hospital spokesperson who declined to be identified provided the information. The more you get involved in writing, the easier it is to acquire sources who will be able to give you the facts as they are.

In addition to checking your facts, be sure to get everyone's name spelt correctly, as well as their titles, when you are quoting someone or writing about someone. At another meeting, I referred to one of the trustees of the town by his nickname. Although it was obvious that it was a nickname, I never followed up with him to ask his real name. My editor caught it, put his real first name, the nickname in quotes, and his last name in the paper.

Checking your facts may seem time-consuming, but it is essential for good journalism. Once you start writing inaccurate accounts, spelling people's names wrong and providing the public with false information, not only your credibility will suffer, but the credibility of the newspaper as well. I was lucky as my editor gave me a second chance.

3. Unbiased. As a human being, it can be difficult to write from an unbiased perspective, but this is good journalism. Today, much journalism is biased to one side or the other and this is becoming more acceptable in the industry. But consider both Fox News and MSNBC. One is biased towards the right and the other the left - do you rely on either of them to tell you about the news from an unbiased perspective? And what does that say about their journalism tactics? It causes most people to distrust them. While one of these 24-hour news channels may be saying what you want to hear, you still want the facts so that you can make up your mind. Good journalism presents the facts in an article and then allows the reader to form their own opinion.

This is easier said than done. I've broken this rule several times throughout the years. But it's bad journalism. One time I covered a zoning board meeting where an elderly couple complained about their property being messed up by the village after a rezoning that the village agreed to in order to accommodate a big builder.

From my perspective, it looked like two David's going after a bunch of Goliaths. And I wrote the article from my perspective. This went over well with the couple who were interested in getting their property restored, but it didn't go over well with my editor who, although printing the story, told me to get facts from both sides, and he emphasized "both sides" at the next meeting. I just interviewed the couple after the meeting and not the planning commissioners. It was biased journalism.

Fortunately, it worked out for the couple whose property was damaged and they got the village to repair the property. But regardless of the outcome, I still wrote a piece of biased journalism. Although the couple was happy, the zoning board was not. Those who gave me tips and information stopped doing so.

While I'm not saying that anyone should sell out to get a source in journalism, you do need to print both sides of the story, regardless of how you feel. Do not attach yourself to your sources so that you become their crusader. It is not your job to be judge and jury - you simply must present the facts to the readers. You are not on one side or another - that is why the press is called the *Fourth Estate*. They are separate entity that does not take sides.

Again, this is easier said than done. But it can be accomplished if you remember to give the same amount of time to both sides in controversy for any article and keep your distance from all sources. Never put yourself in a position where you are writing slanted articles so that you can procure the favour of one side or another. You are a professional who wants, as Joe Friday on Dragnet used to say, "just the facts."

As a human being, you naturally want to help right a wrong, but this is not your job as a reporter. If you feel strongly about a situation, become an activist. Using your position as a journalist to sway the public is not what good journalism is about. Being unbiased will add to your credibility as a journalist, as well as the credibility of the media for whom you write.

Other rules of journalism include not falling in love with your writing and quoting your sources. You cannot just write an article and not quote anyone or refer to a source of information. You are reporting the news. You should always have an "according to" or a quote from a source when you are writing news.

When you are writing features, such as a travel article or an article about an event that comes to town, you have more leeway when it comes to using your perspective. You can give feature articles a bit of panache by writing your own impression, but you still need to quote others who are either natives, experts, or organizers when you write a piece of feature journalism.

For example, if you go to Africa and have to report on conditions in Kenya, you can write about your impression, but also need to quote those who live there or are working there in order to give your article some credence. It is more important that you give the perspective of others in your features than your own. You can make your writing more descriptive, but it should still be in the third person and about other people instead of yourself. There are exceptions to this rule. War correspondents will often write journal-like articles about what they are seeing. This type of correspondent journalism, however, is not what you will most likely be doing when you start in the field. Those journalists who write such compelling pieces got their start writing news stories.

Part of your job as a journalist is to acquire sources. You want to be friendly to them and thank them for their information. In some cases, such as those where they can lose their job or worse if they go on the record, you should protect them. The more sources trust you, the more information they will give you.

Do you pay a source for information? Not unless you plan on working for the National Enquirer or one of the similar tabloids. Good journalists do not pay for information. The reason that tabloids get the "inside story" a great deal of the time is because they pay for information. This backfires on them because they are often tricked by fake sources who will provide them with false information just to make a few dollars. Paying for information is very unprofessional and can ruin your credibility as a journalist. Look at the National Enquirer - do you trust what they tell you? Compare them to the Wall Street Journal - a paper that has not changed its format since inception. Which would you most likely believe?

Another rule is that you do not fall in love with your work. Later, we will discuss copy editors and their jobs. Some journalists go on to be copy editors as well as editors of papers. They will often change your articles without your knowing it. There have been times, especially when I was first starting, that I looked at an article and saw my name in the byline, but the changes made it impossible to recognize as my own.

Needless to say, I found this to be very disappointing. It felt a bit like cheating in that the article was not my own and had my name on it. It hurt my feelings as well. But I soon got used to it. Although I rarely have anything changed today, it happened quite frequently when I began in the field of journalism. My editor soon got used to my writing style and I soon got used to what he wanted. But it still stung.

If you are going to be a journalist, you are going to need some thick skin. If you cannot take criticism of your writing, you are in the wrong field. My writing gets criticized all the time, by other colleagues as well as readers. In the beginning, my editor criticized my writing. I was a bit thin-skinned when I began in this field but soon learned to roll with the punches. If you are going to be overly sensitive about your writing, you seriously need to look for another job other than journalism.

Do not be surprised if you break a few of the rules of journalism along the way - it happens. Be sure to learn from your mistakes and do not make them again as you navigate your way through the world of journalism.

CHAPTER FOUR

Building a Portfolio

Earlier, we talked about a portfolio and how important it is to have one. Your education will not get you in the door unless you have some experience to back it up. Fortunately, there are ways we discussed that will enable you to write even if you do not have your degree and get your name out there.

There are two ways to build a portfolio of your writing samples and you should use both if you are going to look for jobs in journalism. Just like a resume, the portfolio needs to be updated often. You never know when you are going to need to look for a job, so it makes sense to have a resume and portfolio ready to go.

The two ways that you need to use to build a portfolio are to have a printed portfolio as well as a website. Both can aid you in getting a job. You should have both as one is a fast way to show prospective employers your work, and one is more reliable as the printed work will remain even if the website goes down.

Having a website as a portfolio of your work is not difficult. There are many different web hosting companies that will provide free hosting or hosting for a few dollars a month. You do not need a lot of bells and whistles for your website. You just need to have samples of your writing in a professional display. You should have both the writing copied and pasted on your website as well as a link to the live article. Be sure to state that you are including these as samples of your writing so that you do not face copyright infringement in cases where you sold your article to a website.

Only include articles with bylines when you are building a portfolio. Ghostwriting does not count. And for good measure, be sure that you only include articles for which you were paid if you are posting online articles into your portfolio. If you were not paid and put articles on a site like E-zine, you can include them as they, and other article distribution sites will make sure that the article does not contain errors and is well written before they agree to post it.

You will also want to print any articles out that are online under your byline and put them in a folder. But all your articles, clippings and writing samples in a professional-looking portfolio so that you can present it to a prospective employer.

Write as much as you can, take on jobs as a stringer or even write for free to build your portfolio. The internet has made it easier than ever to get a byline for your work, although it is good if you have some print media included in your portfolio along with internet articles.

Regarding your website, be sure that it is professional and depicts your updated resume. You can easily apply for a job by sending a link to your website to an employer. You should also upload a resume for them to look at so they can view that before they opt to go to your website. Having a website can enable you to not only get internet writing jobs but also print media jobs as today everyone wants to get information as fast as possible. Having a professional website as well as a printed, professional portfolio is one way that you can impress potential employers and land a job in the journalism field.

CHAPTER FIVE

What Is Style?

Style allows for all writing to be consistent. There are two main style guides that most papers use. They are the *Associated Press Style Guide* and the *Chicago Style Guide*. They have to do with using commas, what to capitalize, writing out numbers and other matters of form. Any media should use the same style as it makes everything more consistent and easier to read. Here is an example of a poor style:

On Friday, April 23, 2008, John Smith stole 12 oranges from Gallo's Supermarket. Smith was arrested and detained on three charges for stealing the twelve oranges. In addition to oranges, Smith also stole apples, tomatoes, and pears.

Henry Gallo, owner of Gallo's supermarket stated that he saw Smith look at the oranges, apples, tomatoes, and pears and looked like he was considering theft. He watched him pick up 3 apples but put them down. Then he stole the twelve oranges.

You can get the picture. The story does not use commas, capitalization, or numbers consistently. This is just an example of style and how it works. It can be difficult to read an article that is not consistent when it comes to style. Nothing is wrong with the facts of the article, but it is difficult to read because it does not follow a certain type of style.

If you are in college, you are most likely being taught a different style of writing than you learned in high school. Some colleges have their style guides. Many writing jobs, especially those online, will not want two spaces after a period. This is standard when you are learning how to type, or keyboard as it is now called, but many online outlets do not want the two spaces after the end of a sentence. This is for space reasons and is also a style issue.

Commas are very subjective, although some people go a little comma happy and use them too often. Some do not use them at all. Commas break up a train of thought in a sentence. For the most part, it is difficult to say what is right or what is wrong. But when it comes to writing for print media or online, you need to understand their style manual so that you know how to use commas as well as other elements of style.

Many copy editors will go over the style for you and make corrections. But it is important to learn about writing styles and what to use when you are writing for any company. While you are in school, you will most likely be taught the *Associated Press* style as this has become the most accepted style.

Learning style points is not difficult. At first, if you are used to using a certain type of style, you may find that it is hard to change the way that you are used to writing based on a new style guide, but as you continue writing, you will find that it gets easier and become more natural. To pursue a career in journalism, you are going to have to be flexible when it comes to style and be careful to use it according to the style manual used by the company for which you work.

One way to brush up on your style is to pay close attention to the details given to you when it comes to turning in college essays. Most college professors will mark off for style errors, especially if you are a journalism major. While some writers do not like this bit of detail, it is crucial to understand style, why it is used and how to use it for your own writing. Again, the more you get used to the style, the more natural writing using a certain style will come to you. It may take a bit of effort at first, but it will soon become second nature to you.

CHAPTER SIX

What Does a Copy Editor Do?

A copy editor goes over your work, corrects style errors and makes sure there are no grammatical errors or spelling. In some cases, especially when you are first starting, the copy editor will rewrite certain parts of your story. They will make sure that the article makes sense and conforms to the media for which it is written.

Many papers today are asking writers to do their own copy editing. This is the same when it comes to some online venues. As news and entertainment media are trying to trim their budgets, many are cutting out copy editing as much as possible.

A rival newspaper to the one for which I work is now asking reporters to do their own copy editing for any weekend stories. This is expected to increase over time as the newspaper is down in circulation and has laid off a great deal of their staff. It is good for any writer who wants a career in journalism to know about copy editing not only for the sake of the media for which they write but also to make their articles look more professional.

Copy editors also will give a title to an article. While you may like a certain title, it may not be catchy enough or fit with the publication. A great deal of the job of a copy editor is to make sure that the article catches the eye of the reader.

There are several avenues that a journalist can take when they want to move up in the career field. While some prefer just to write and seek out better assignments, others enjoy editing. If you have a good eye for detail, you may consider copy editing your work and pursuing this field. This is one career in journalism that pays well and can be used for many other purposes. You can move up this ladder and eventually become an editor or even the editor in chief of the paper.

A copy editor does not only have to know good journalism skills but also have a thorough knowledge of the style manual being used by the publication and excellent grammatical skills. Many writers avoid details like the black plague because they tend to bog them down and can stifle creativity. However, these details are an important aspect of putting out any sort of readable material. All writers should learn to copy edit as much of their work as possible.

When you first begin writing, the articles that you write will have to be rewritten as it is difficult to get to the point where an article comes out of your head and onto paper without revisions. As you continue to write, however, you will find that it becomes easier.

Here are a few tips on how to copy edit your articles:

1. Check for style and make sure that it is consistent throughout the article.

2. Go on a "witch hunt" and eliminate "which" when you can use "that".

3. Proof for errors in spelling by reading each line from the end to the beginning to make sure you are not skipping over anything.

4. Proof for consistency in what you are stating in your article.

5. Avoid any awkward sentences or phrases.

6. Avoid clichés.

7. Try to come up with a title that will make readers want to read the story.

If you do this and then read over your article again, you can copy edit your work. The more you get used to doing this, the better your chances are of turning in polished and professional work to your editor.

At the very least, be sure to check your facts, name spellings and read over your piece for any errors in grammar or spelling before turning it into your editor. If you habitually turn in sloppy pieces of material that make the copy editor work overtime, you can end up losing your job. Sure, you are under the gun and need to make a deadline. But that is no excuse for turning in work that is full of errors.

As you will most likely be writing your articles on a computer, use a word processing program that will give you grammatical corrections as well as offer spell check and even auto-correct to streamline the process. Do not rely solely on the computer to do your work for you, though. Still take the time to read it through and make sure it makes sense before turning it into your editor.

Whether or not your publication has a copy editor or not, do not put the entire burden of correcting your work on him or her. Take pride in what you write and make sure that it is polished and professional before you turn it in for publication.

CHAPTER SEVEN

Additional Degrees to Consider

After you have achieved your BA in journalism, you may want to consider furthering your education. You can choose to embark on getting a post-graduate degree and get a Master's degree in Arts if you want to open more doors for yourself. These days, a Bachelor's degree is like a high school diploma used to be 20 years ago. If you want to go far in any career field, you should consider getting a post-graduate degree in that field, including journalism.

You can also further your education by getting a degree in other fields that are related to journalism. If you have always dreamed of a job in front of a camera and want to be a television reporter, you need to look for a degree in broadcasting. You can then apply to work at a television station as a writer and wait for your big break as a broadcast reporter. You will need to have not only the knowledge on how to effectively report the news but also how to broadcast it so that others will pay attention.

If you get a following as a television news reporter, chances are that you will be asked to substitute for anchors who are out sick occasionally. This can lead to a full-time stint as an anchorperson. Many of those who are anchors today began working as news reporters. Not all just went into broadcasting careers from college. If you enjoy reporting and like being in front of a camera, you should seek out a journalism career that puts you at a TV station. With the advent of 24-hour news stations that continue to expand, there is more of a need than ever for those who not only know about journalism but broadcasting as well.

Anchor persons today do not write their own copy. A copywriter will write the copy for them to read, and they will read it from the teleprompter. This skill is taught in broadcasting school. In addition to broadcasting on TV, you might also want to consider broadcasting on radio. These are all offshoots of careers in journalism. If there is any reporting to be done, even broadcasting majors must know the fundamentals of journalism.

Another degree you may want to pursue is teaching. A great deal of those who pursue careers in journalism will study for a teaching certificate so that they can either make extra money teaching the course, or they can have a less hectic life. After many years in the field of journalism, some people look for a change of pace. Teaching is one of the ways that people can make use of their journalism degree.

When you first start as a journalist, especially if you plan on working for a newspaper, you cannot expect to earn much money. The money comes as you continue down the career path and add knowledge, experience, and more skills to your resume. A career in journalism should never be stagnant. You should be seeking to learn new experiences and gain as much knowledge as you can when it comes to this field.

The more you pursue higher forms of education as well as dabble in other areas of the field, the more experience you will gain, and the more doors will be open to you. If you are considering a career in the field of journalism, you should back it up with a minor in broadcasting, a teaching certificate or be prepared to take additional courses so that you can grow to the heights you want in this exciting career field.

CHAPTER EIGHT

Online Journalism

Online journalism is the way of the future and needs to be acknowledged by anyone who is seriously considering pursuing a career in this field. Many traditional newspapers are having a hard time maintaining their circulation since people can get their news right on the internet, and much quicker than they could if they waited for the latest edition of the paper. We are gradually moving towards the internet for the latest news and the traditional newspapers are being left in the dust.

This does not mean that there is not a calling for print media and those who want to work for a paper or a magazine. Although people can get news quicker on the internet than they can with a newspaper, people still like to have something tangible to hold. Magazines are not suffering as much as newspapers when it comes to circulation.

There is one way that you can take advantage of the fact that many newspapers are dropping their full-time staff and that is to become a freelance journalist. You can write for more than one outlet in this way, especially if you are writing for online media. Most internet news media hires freelancers instead of full-time staff. Freelance journalism over the internet is one way to find a career in the field of journalism and get paid for writing.

There is one caveat to becoming a freelance journalist online, however. That is that the online media is not taken as seriously as print media. Even though the print media seems to be diminishing, they are still considered the top dog when it comes to writing. The internet news venues are like poor relations compared to the larger news conglomerates. Still, online writing is the way of the future, and many experts predict that we will see much fewer newspapers in ten years.

You can get started working as a freelancer at an online news network by applying. You will apply electronically just as you would for an offline job. You also want to be sure that you send an updated resume and portfolio. This is when your website will come in handy. If you get a job as an online freelancer, chances are that you will work from your home and be given assignments. Depending on the outlet for which you work, you may or may not be given enough work to make a living. The good news is that as a freelancer, you are not committed to any outlet. You can moonlight at other publications and, if you do not copy your own material, you can make a living in journalism right from your own home.

Another positive aspect of online journalism writing is that it may not require a degree. You can get started by applying for different jobs at any online news media site that you see.

The negative aspect of being an online freelancer is that you do not have the same job security as you would have if you worked offline. Websites come and go frequently, and you may end up with the short end of a stick if you choose one that ends up folding, especially if they owe you money. Another negative aspect about an online job is that there are many unscrupulous companies out there that will take your work and not pay you.

Some will even offer to pay you by page views. I ran into one company that said they were going to be a formidable force online and wanted experienced and educated writers that would write news columns for them for free, in exchange for getting page views. They did not tell me of this rule until I was ready to sign up. I demurred and decided to stick with the job I still have, and I am glad I did. Not only did I get the column that I wanted at my current job, but I have yet to see anything about this site that promised to "take over the internet" with their news stories.

All journalists should look to the internet as a potential career move. In addition, right now it is a smart choice to work as a freelancer in this field as there are many more opportunities open to you both online and offline.

Look to make about $50 an article when you are starting. I have found this to be true both online and offline. Most freelancers are paid a flat fee for their articles, and it is usually in this range. Remember if you are freelancing, either online or offline that you need to put some money away for taxes. You can fill out a Schedule C for your income taxes and pay a self-employment tax for what you make. If you do decide to go the freelance route, as many journalists are doing, be sure to have a good accountant who will be able to advise you on what type of deductions you can take on your income taxes.

Both online writing, as well as freelancing, are ways of the future when it comes to the field of journalism. If you are going to pursue a career in this field, chances are that you are going to start in one or the other - or both. Have an open mind and make sure that any online sources that recruit you are willing to pay you for your articles. Just say "no" to those that promise page view money as your only compensation, even if they are planning on "taking over the internet."

CHAPTER NINE

What to Expect on Your First Job

When you get your first job as a journalist, do not expect to make much money. I have already told you about my first job. Although I stayed with the paper after graduation and was brought into the office as a full-time employee, I still wasn't making much money. I found out that everyone in the newsroom was in the same boat. Journalism, at least on the smaller scale levels, does not pay very well.

Newspaper reporters can make a living, but not expect to make good money unless they become editors or columnists. Columnists have to then be syndicated or have a strong following to make a decent living. Becoming a columnist takes time and you must pay your dues by writing as a reporter until you get your break.

You may decide to stick with your first job or just build a resume and move on. If you want to grow, you should keep your portfolio and resume updated and continue to look for better opportunities. The type of opportunities that you seek out depends on the results you expect to attain in your career. As is the case with following other career paths, you need to set a long-term goal for yourself as well as short term goals on how you can get to where you want to be.

Your long-term goal may be to be an editor of a paper, work on a magazine or be a television reporter. If so, then you are only likely to achieve one of them by working as a newspaper reporter. But, again (and I can't say this enough) working as a newspaper reporter is the best on the job training that you can get if you want to pursue a career in journalism or any career in writing. It teaches you to write fast, think fast and meet deadlines. Your writing skills will improve dramatically when you work in this field. Unless you want to stay with the newspaper and become an editor or columnist, you may want to use the newspaper as a steppingstone.

If you like being a newspaper reporter and are happy with this type of job, there is no reason to change. Some are content with working at local papers and being close to home. They get to know their community and can eventually move up in the company where they started.

As for me, I was not the type who wanted to be an editor. I don't have the eye for fine details. I liked my job reporting and my goal was to become a columnist for the paper. I finally achieved my goal earlier this year after taking 6 years to get there. I got the job when the columnist we had retired. Instead of applying for the job through the normal channels, I wrote a column so that the editor could see what I did. You will find that in the journalism field, you need to take action.

You may not have any idea what you want to do in the long term as you begin your career in journalism. That is fine, too. You should work in your field and get as much experience as possible so that you can broaden your horizons and decide what you want to do. Even if you opt for just staying local as a news reporter, you should at least know what else is out there.

By continuing to gain experience, build a portfolio and take additional schooling, you can rise to the level you desire in the field of journalism. One thing to remember - Journalism is a very competitive field. If there is a job that you want, you must take action to try to get it. This is not a field for shrinking violets.

Chances are that your first job in journalism will lead to many others and that this is just the start of an exciting career in the field of journalism. If you are competitive, willing to work hard and learn about the field of journalism, you will find much success when you choose this as your career, no matter what your long-term goal is for your future.

Good luck in pursuing your career in journalism. Remember, you do not have to be Hemingway to make a living at writing. There are plenty of ways to make money when pursuing a journalism career, especially if you are open to the internet or freelance writing.

Printed by Libri Plureos GmbH in Hamburg,
Germany